Solitary Man

Street Fame Books
SFB
Hollywood, CA
www.streetfamebooks.com

For my brother John

Who I wanted to be like so much
when I was a teenager growing up
with his long hair and wild mind.

Sometimes I feel like I'm chasing my dreams
for the both of us.

ALSO BY

ROBERT PAUL TAYLOR

DRIFTING

LIKE THIS

ALL OUT WAR

OF EVERYTHING I ONCE LOVED

IMPASSE

ITHICA

SKYLINE

THE GARDEN

ONE NIGHT STAND

SOLITARY MAN

FIRST EDITION PRINTED
SEPTEMBER 2015

CHARLES WINTHROP WETHERFORD
FOREVER

COVER PHOTO:
GARRET SUHRIE COPYRIGHT 2015

BORN, BLED & PRINTED IN THE GOOD OLE U.S.A

"Belinda was mine, til the time
that I found her, loving Jim.
Then Sue came along, loved me strong
that's what I thought, me and Sue.
But that died too..."

-John Cash

The Clothes in the Cabinets

FORWARD

I keep waiting for that singular moment to happen.
That deep, moving, spiritual shift in perception. That one moment
when you find yourself exactly in a place you couldn't have imag-
ined distracted by the peripheral noise of the current scene and you
are just being.

Simultaneously processing hundreds of threads from past mo-
ments, when suddenly, pieces of stories rearrange inside your mind.
Resentments magically dissipate, the limb of memory twists and
your emotional radar elevates. You feel something bright orange
and warm deep inside your chest expanding outwards.
You experience that tiny drop of serotonin. There is a deep angelic
comfort in the whole journey.

Everything makes sense.

There has been a shift in your perception and suddenly you can see behind you and in front of you clearly. You are surrounded by gratitude in a soft blanket of thanksgiving. Overwhelming joy floods over yourself, the brow unfurrows, your shoulders relax and the lungs exhale a calming sigh of victory.

Pure bliss in your existence on planet earth.

Some call this a 'spiritual awakening'.

Some people call it a moment of bliss.

Our sweat leader Wolf, who pours the lodge ceremonies calls this moment 'our natural state'.

"These subtle and in frequent moments of bliss, are really our natural state of being", strong jawed he slowly mentions muffled through an American Spirit cigarette with a native tongue, long silver hair braided down his back in a kneeling position in front of the fire.

Just for a moment, we are able to see above all the things that we've stacked upon ourselves. Just for a moment, we can see what and who we really are. The place we hold here on Turtle Island, as they call it on the Red Road. The place we hold here in this human realm.

These are the small moments I have been trying to expand upon. To recreate them. To find them again, in the jungles of our minds so to speak.

I recently was reading an article on the largest cave in the world named 'Son Doong' near the Laos-Vietnam border.
A poor local Vietnamese man named Ho Kanh discovered the magical cave in 1991.

Ho and his family were very poor villagers and part of his survival routine to help sustain his family would be to go deep into the jungles in search of firewood and eventually further in deeper, in search of Aloe.

The resin of Aloe is used to make perfume and is very valuable. Yet so many would never go that deep into the jungle because of the wildlife and its terrain.

One particular journey, Ho had gone further than he ever had before and a tremendous storm had come overhead as he scurried for shelter from the torrential downpour.

He sat down with his back to a huge boulder.

Then something strange happened. He heard the sound of a strong wind and water running behind him through the large rock.

He further investigated around and finally came to an opening in the wall. Inside he found an entrance to an enormous cave, with a wide river flowing out of it. In the pitch dark, he said he 'felt like he was walking into a huge space, a strong wind that felt like something from the underworld".

The next day he arrived home. He didn't have any Aloe, but in his mind he had the image of a great cave.

Kanh's story spread like wildfire in the village, but not everyone believed him.

He wanted to prove himself to the others.

The only problem was that he could not find the cave again. He searched for years, and years. He could not find his way back to the place he found his excitement.

15 years later a British team flew to Vietnam and hired Ho to trek with them in search of the cave that was now a legend.

The team searched for extensive periods of time spanning years with no luck.

In a final effort to recover his memory, Ho set out to the jungle one cold winters morning in 2009.

This time, he found his cave again.

The British team immediately came back to Vietnam to document and explore the cave that had never been touched by human hands.

The cave itself is large enough to fit entire city streets and skyscrapers. Millions of years of water carving over limestone have created beautiful and unbelievable formations.

Occasional collapses in the roof have allowed underground jungle ecosystems to form, and with them, all-new species that have never been seen anywhere else. Rare cave pearls, ancient fossils, and towering stalactites form around a river running through the caves so large that they even have their own clouds.

All from these 'occasional collapses' in the roof that allowed the sun to shine through sharing some of that beautiful photosynthesis for life to form.

These are the 'occasional collapses' that I keep searching for.

The places where I can feel the ceiling break away just a bit, and a healing ray of light shines through.
More flora. More tiny little ferns. More light.

We need more light.

I have moments like this in Native American ceremony.

Inside the altar, the lodge, it is pitch black once we get inside and close the door.

Sometimes deep in the third round, I can look up and see the stars. I can see my father, my friends. I see animals. I see shooting stars. Problems solve themselves. Past relationships become guide points.

The humming beating of the drum, powerful Lakota prayer songs, the sweat dripping down my face & my back become the ingredients.

There is no light shinning through. But when the stone people are hot enough, when the drum beats loud & the prayers lift strong enough, the light shines through all right.

I don't know how, I don't know when, but it does.

I think we are all searching for our Son Doong cave.

We have laid our backs upon it once. We have gone back to the places we once were before. Yet somehow the scenery was different.

I believe that's truly what drug addiction is all about. On a deep emotional level it's about going back to the cave entrance. Not giving up on finding the way back. Unfortunately, our human bodies give up before our minds do, and hence the tragedies in life.

What if we could find our way back? What if we could stay there forever? What if we could share the path with others? What if we could build our lives around this special place? What if we found this place, and we decided not to leave? Is that what monks are doing in their journey? Is that what the men and women of cloth are leading? Did they find their home and hath not left?

I am heading back to the rich green jungles of Thailand again this year to join the Buddhist Monks in the Temple of Doisuthep, high up in the mountains of Chiang Mai.

The temple is the grandest of all temples, draped in gold statues with rows of tiny burning oil lamps, candles dripping, incense smoldering and marble floors stretching out past what feels like city blocks.

Ancient maps on the walls, smooth cold pillars, painted voyages across continents adorn hallways, huge golden Buddha's lined in formation, terra cotta roofs, beautifully rusted copper trim.

The entire Temple sits atop of a huge mountain with a view of the Old Town below and the vast countryside that envelops every corner.

Only the monks live there. At nighttime, the night jungle winds gently blow the temple bells to an ancient golden jingle sound that literally harmonizes ones soul. The sight of incense sticks burning in the wind with no one around is something of spirit magic.

Beautiful temple dogs sleep quietly in corners. The passing of an old Monk in the hallway is occasional, but usually the whole place is empty, beautifully light in the golden reflection of the moonlight, somehow, hundreds of years later, still simmering away in the jungles of Thailand's ancient capital.

During the retreat it is required to wear all white garments, eat two vegan meals a day and pray and mediate for up to 12 hours a day with an hour of group chanting in the evening.

We do not speak to each other for a week. You learn the meaning of useless talking and just how much we really don't need to say. But more importantly, this teaches you that when you do speak, it can be beautiful.

There is no such thing as an uncomfortable silence in ceremony. Only a peaceful one.

Just enough food to meditate. Just enough sleep to pray.

At night time, I walk up the long stairs that trace the steep hillside of the mountain. I let my bare feet slip over hundreds of years old marble floors, pass countless decades of prayers, with the smell of incense and the chime of temple bells to the wind.

I find a place in one of the corners, settle myself and close my eyes.

I am packing my bag again.
Water, food, prayer and a hopeful outlook.
I am heading out one more time.

I'm going to find that cave entrance again.

I know I will.

-Robert Paul Taylor
August 31, 2015

The Six And The Nine

And because it has been so long
So many nights I have seen
Under the same darkened sky

Under the same savoring healing sun
The same rushing streets
Of the city we both share
It is all of these sleepless nights
That lead us

As the rain falls & your arms in mine
I feel like you have already saved me
In the knick of time
I feel like you are already sharing
A slice of this fragile shine

Scaring you a bit when I stop
& just stare
I can't help but lose my words
Swallow my tongue
And just gaze into the eyes
Of your world

So fragile & delicate
You have the presence of the world
God uniting us both
It was in prayer that I first found you
12/11/09

The House On The Hill

It was the most favored month
Of a snow covered year
The skies fled
To ashes, I bled
The nights away without you

New found love
We found that place
Searching
For so long
Once touched, but
Never quite held
It's you, now that I pray
My faith has guided

Through the tree's we walk
Under the cloud's crying eyes
In the dark of the night
Together
We melt into the seats
Of my car
Steaming up windows
Staring
Stretching faces
Emotional reflections
The journey we have run

Never walked
Always ran
It has only been hours since this began
With you and I
And I already can feel
The presence of you and I
And God and love and bountiful fever
I give it all away

To have someone to come home to

So like I always have
I know how to do this
Be patient
And willing
And loving
And kind
Say my prayers
For you and mine

And come Tuesday
Into your arms eyes and soul
Will I fall so grace full

Waiting for you to come
My newfound love
Waiting to find
This new beautiful
Ocean of serenity we have began
The house on the hill
The place you take me
The moment I see your eyes
12/12/09

Interruption In Stagnation

God I am so giddy
Thank you for your shield
Of faith and love
Your guidance
From above
Thank you for
All the gifts
You have so freely
Given to me

Just like the darkness
Falling victim to light
She came to me last night
It held us so tight
In each others arms
The energy surrounded
Us like a force field
With faith
We heal
Each other first
Then the world
Making something
Great of this life
I want it all
Under your guidance
And not mine
Today I am so
Grateful
For every sleepless
Night alone
Every crying whisper
Through the phone
For my time to reveal
To harness my warrior
Is here and now

She told me
This is dreamtime baby
The whole package
So here I sign my name
My blood and spit
Challenge myself
To change
To cause some interruption
In stagnation
Cause the pain nation
To reveal our true selves
You inspire me to perspire
You inspire me to heal
Just put your little hand in mine
And together we can
Walk the rest of the way home
12/11/09

I Was Invisible

Higher frequency all day
Higher frequently
There is no other way
To lift myself out of bed
Just to hit my knees
I plead with thanksgiving
And gratitude
This plentitude of opportunities
Overwhelms me when I think
Of everything at once
So it is in prayer
That I just see you

Getting ready mentally
To let you into this home
The cobwebs have overgrown
And now I must make the changes
My father once told me of

The way a woman checks the nest
Leaves her scent
Where she stops to rest
For the night
Oh my tap water
I worry

Through December there is no hurry
For this is my time of the year
I attract what I need
And only that may stay
Circling like a cyclone
My whole world
I built alone
With you god

Revving like an engine
Strong centered and focused
Still alone jumping like
A thousand locusts
I devour the future
Loving the suture's of life
And my scars, so many lessons
Everything I once loved
Has brought me forward
Making the pages I am today
Freeing the man I appear
Before your eyes
Like a prayer I was invisible

The rains came
And you fell from the sky
Through my fingers
And through my eyes
Pushing forward this inertia
Of faith and love
No need to beg, borrow
Or steal
For this life is my meal
And I eat so well

My sister told me yesterday
That I have saved enough
Young girls
It's time for teacher-teacher
So preacher-preacher
Send me a teacher
Someone I can spill this goblet
Of energy with
Someone to slip in
This abundance

A strong god centered woman

I can take my perfect circle
And make a perfect circle
For I am whole, perfect and complete
On my own
But boy we sure do
Smash together well
Like well done mash potato's
I want to gum drop
Your little hand in mine
Speed off, get lost in time
Lets take a long flight
Take a long swim
Sit together on the mountain
And just pray

Lets jump some continents
The whole world to play
My ego wants to talk
But with love I say shush
For no reason to push
For I am not in control
I surrender my self with
With adaptability
And flexibility to reveal

As the snow falls in Idaho
Just know that it falls in
My mind as well
And only time
She can always tell

This plentitude of opportunities
Overwhelms me when I think
Of everything at once
So it is in prayer
That I just see you

12/13/09

8

Years Of Catharsis

And so you cast this spell
Over me
Or was it just a rainy night
That made, everything right
I have so much faith in myself
& the feeling when I know
It's right
Yet there's that fear
Late at night
Creeping on a bike
That sometimes wants to
Stand & block light
Causing an angelic eclipse
Of reality, bliss
Confusing, the way
The water falls to the ground
Watching puddles
Hearing sounds
Sit alone & walk
Through the month
Remember this is still
About God
Always about trust
In you
Faith
& the way home
Hard to not put so much
Weight on your shoulders so fast
I can view the history
Often ran out of gas
Suppose it makes sense
To go easy on the pedal
Holding back in ways
Would rather just punch it
But that's what I always do

And then it's only in the kitchen
Where I only see you
Just sitting here alone
Typing away
Filling pages of books
No one seems to read
Healing myself
From my own self inflicted need
Of needing something
Someone

My mother told me today
To be careful not to smother you
How could she say something
So relevant and we never even
See each other
She knows me without seeing
Me, I was born from her flesh
Her mind, must be like mine
At times such a mess
Oh mother I must confess
Sometimes I want to blame
This all on you

Been difficult not to smoke
So many years of catharsis
My last real vice
Finally the time to kick
Chewing so much gum
Seems to work for now

Still in the kitchen writing
Always
Pondering
Knowing something is coming
I just wish it would hurry up
12/15/09

10

Deep Under The Sea

Walking again-
Seems like we just keep
Holding and talking
Eyes and hands like stone
Somehow
Somewhere alone
Some pitchfork in the road
Aimed us together
Someone from above
Sent us this weather
And so together again
When the sky turned to black
You came back
To breath
To love
Teaching me now

In the physical form
The most beautiful thing
I might have just ever seen
Eyes like the Grand Canyon
Delicate ears
Perfect posture
Perfect sheen
Dancing like a queen
We walk for hours yet
Never seem to get far
Too far from our zone
Domestic Cancer
Keeping protected
We stay close to home

My feet dance and my heart
Beats, but its just my eyes
That meet

Yours and truly
I would do anything
In this moment

There's a fire burning inside
That I just don't care
About running-
Or hiding-
Or acting or retracting
I just want to make a shelter
On the hill
And keep you safe tonight
I'll light the fire
And keep the light
Just teach me how to love again

Show me how
Shine even brighter
Burning eyes like a fighter
My love I challenge
You so
I take your hand slow
And whisper words to myself
That you are just not ready
To hear yet

Watching your pig tails
At your side
I am trying so dam hard
Not to look down at your thighs
But like a garbage disposal
Darling I want to destroy you
In the most loving way
Moving furniture around
The room
In the distance I can hear the boom
Of you and I creating

Something powerful
Some enigma of love
An entire ocean of white doves
Floating for the sunrise

For everything that is mine
I ask for no mercy this time
For there has never been something
Quite like this
For I have never been as centered as
I am today
I am okay
I am willing
And ready
And loving
And steady

You have become my equal
And it is you that you see in me
Nothing else can free me
As does your loving key
So show no mercy for me
Even when I'm down on my knees

For nothing can hurt us
Not another 1000 nights alone
Even as the humming gets louder
This vibration pulls
Just take my hand little one
Looking straight into you
As we just keep walking
Through this force field
12/17/09

The Sky And The Land

Taking us to that place
To watch souls disappear
Like you said
Something I needed you to see
A place to repent
A place to be free
The sweats
My sacred tented
Dome, sleepless
And alone
But now it is you
Whose head I cradle
So rich a
Ladle full of cream
Pouring love
Over the mountains
And hills, in my dreams
Swimming, the darkness
Everything flies

Just your hand in mine
The sweat chases
These scars away
Running them across the street
Epidermis peel
The heat making
Us heal
From sickness
& strife
The delicate crystal
Glass of life
With thick
Pure warrior
Blue blood
I put on these boxing gloves

& take another bow, towards love
For I have not seen you for years
In fact, with these new eyes
& these new ears
I have never seen you before
Quite like this at all

Wasn't it just the fall
Where I was praying to be born
And now, the first day of winter
The longest night of the year
Stretching romantic shears
To toss & tumble
Into leaves
Rolling around black seas
Sheets & lips
Fingers

& hips
& touching
Your breath
My neck
You jump
I call
Together we
Fall, into the darkness
Blending our lines
So the future
We make our own colors

Blurring our clothes
Let the things
That don't work between
Us slide off the wing
Of the plane
This newest game plan
The sky and the land

I have waited for this night
Target practice for years
Finally an equal in sight
And sound

Loving you on the ground
Rolling around the bed
Or was it the living room
Or the car-
Suddenly the ceilings ajar
Take it slow baby
For I have no where to rush
Fingers in your mouth
To hush you

Waking in & out
Of consciousness
Of dreamscapes
& movie scenes
Fall into your neck
The glass of water
On the nightstand
Floats in the air
Rolling over Colorado
The map changes
Shapes at my feet
Cities, below my back
Alarm clock melting
As we wake up on the ceiling

Feet hanging over the door
Lamp shades, ceiling trim
The bed down on the ground
I think were floating in some space
You warm hands on my back
The smell of your hair
Puts me back under

Where I want to be
As my world just spins
Like some slow circus wheel
In one big tumble
Upside down
12/23/09

Crumble

No matter how hard it gets
You got to hold your head up high
Eyes to the sky
Pull that trigger
Shatter the glass
From the past
Let all that cookie
Just crumble
Smashing through streets
So mean
So late at night
We fight to be the best
That we can be
Together
We can be
Together
We are stronger
Than one

12/29/09

Ignorant Falling

Looking over at you
With the silhouette
Of a movie star
Sitting in the movie's
With my 3-D star
Three weeks singing
So far
Been a goner since
The second you stepped
Out of that yellow
Flagged taxicab

You know what I love
About you and I
We just happened
Like burning flames in the sky
Explosions from nowhere
Evolution everywhere
And we just smooth scars
We can sit still
We can sit far
But no matter
What happens today
We just are

I woke up this morning
Realizing you were everywhere
The rains are here again
And you are the sky
The coffee in my mug
You are my mud

Last night you asked
If you could be my guest
Dominican Republic, the best

Just the way you think alone
I think were in the zone

Baby and I want to fall
I have no parachute
No ripcord
I hope you don't mind
If I just eject the front door
Of my mind
Let it all decompress
Letting loose articles
To fly free
And escape the atmosphere
As my hair and jewelry
Just tug at the pressure
As we both step closer
To the edge
This romance war
Smiling so ignorant
Falling so dumb
Halfway leaning
Out of this airplane
Door
So many thousands of
Feet in the air

12/30/09

However far away

I will always love you

Children Will Understand

Swirling hands & arms
Through the inertia
Music to our ears
Pushing the mind
Into complete
Expansion
This mansion
Of everything
I have ever known
Just blown into purple
Radiant flames
& amazes me
In a light show in my mind
With eyes wide open
I see both sides

Walking down these subway stairs
So lost in your current
So lost in your eyes
Embrace me new world
Take me new places
In time
How could there still be
Places I have yet to run
How could I find
Yet another corridor of space
In my mind

Waiting for my subway car to arrive
So far traveled
Dancing in another world
My chemical princess
Something our children will understand
I no longer ask
Now I demand your hand

So lost in your eyes
Last night

Falling through space
Time continuum
Like some falling angelic rhythm
Effervescent colors
Of jellyfish
And satin clouds

Clouding my arms
So safe
In this heat wave
With you
Of mazes
My animal
You are my zoo
The draft blows my scarf
Flirting with my face
Baby you are everywhere
In this place
And I am with you

Let us make love in this den
Take us to another level of Zen
The choir sings me away
Close my eyes
And sway
The subway takes me down
This tube
Of life and memories
Sprawling, crawling
Gasping for air
For your sweat

You're everything true
Tortures me

With lust
Clawing at my cage
Raging
This battle of passion
Aimed at you

Let me eat from your curves
Lay your jawbone
Into my waistline
Become part of my heritage
Like cocktails
Of humanity
Zumanity
Illuminating
Lost in love hallucinating
A fistful of your hair
In my hand
I have returned to primal
My spirit growing
And I don't know how far
I will expand

Now this is high frequency
This is the true hour
Our love is power
Dipping my hands in this current
We are creating
Such a powerful source of light
Of life
Of inspiration
This is the juice of the tree
The beat rocks me
The love I run to
Every night

You are the space I grow towards
Universal freedom

Inside and outside
I no longer believe in time
Headphones blaring
While you just keep blowing my mind

Swirling hands & arms
Through the inertia
Music to our ears
Pushing the mind
Into complete
Expansion
This mansion
Of everything
I have ever known
Just blown into purple
Radiant flames
And amazes me
In a light show in my mind
With eyes wide open
12/30/09

We All Bleed

Blood covered hands
And blood covered hearts
Smearing the covers dark
Together we slip
In the redness of the world
As deep inside
Of you
I am
Together
With the earth
We all bleed

Crunching
And cracking
The sweat and semen
Dry and crack
Every time we lay back
And adjust ourselves
Deeper into this sand box
Of deepened awareness

Sex is a mystery
Love is a mission
Together with maps
And calipers, spyglasses
And leather pouches
We scour the earth
For the sign

Passion, hunter
Ambition, hunger
Splintered with hope
Scratching, leaning
Can't keep this fire silent
As everything we touch

Becomes gold

Everything ever touched
Touched by God
Dripping thighs
Tucked away in your eyes
The force field you keep
Confuses my gauges
So flying blinded by light
Through the darkened sky
High above the clouds
Something pulls

Closer and closer
Reaching for the moon
Sometimes your hands
Reach past this room
And the distance is
Your breath
Every room in the house
Wreaks of you
And your clothes
And clips, and wraps and scents
Like a sidewalk
I litter myself with you

Making it only hours
At most
Until I'm back in your arms
In your chamber again
The only place I feel safe
Refilling and refueling
In mid air we dance
Trance like children
Planting the seeds
Of tomorrow in the dirt
Of today

Praying white chapels
Falling red apples
To the floor together
We go with gravity
We stay so close
During these times
Just holding on tight
For reasons
We just can't seem to grasp

We don't need to
Understand this clasp
Something from a life before
The book of Destiny
That look of intensity
Some kind of cosmic karma
Playing this circle of completion
We meet again
My love

Possibly a second time
Around the globe
The universe needs this
Plot to unfold
For I am the receiver
And you are the giver
I am your heartbeat
You are my liver
Hand in hand
Time spans across land
So much had to happen
To both of us
For this to finally
Happen
To both of us

We drove so far

In so many separate scars
Landscapes of different jars
Through mortar and tar
We shattered and frayed
At the ends

Now so strong
We pull together
Every night in my eyes
I see you in every disguise
The woman from centuries ago
I found you again
Was it Florence or Greece
Romania or Nice
Where we once lived
And livestock in the night
Hid, under sycamores
When the October skies
Turned to Orange
We became something
Grander than the great winter

For the next century to come
This love is ours
And nothing in the Universe
Can stop this
For I am not pulling
Nor pushing
Just my eyes open
I am accepting
For I am the receiver
And you are the giver
I am your heartbeat
You are my liver

Blood covered hands
And blood covered hearts

Smearing the covers dark
Together we slip
In the redness of the world
As deep inside
Of you
I am
Together
With the earth
We all bleed

01/11/10

Sleeping So Free

Coming to a familiar
Place in the road
I have seen this fence
Before
So many times did I
Turn left
And just keep walking
And always ended up
At the burned down
City at the end of line

Too many mistakes
Too many stakes
At risk this time
I been playing for keeps
This far so why
Not take it further
Finally old enough to hold
A flame

Finally bold enough
To walk through the shame
Guilt from the past
Freedom from the pain

So watch me walk
Through this chalk
Line from the past
And keep the beauty
We have cashed
For this time I want

Something different
I want something
Indifferent

I want something
I have never had
So I have to do things
I have never done

And with this chance
I take
I choose truth
The beauty in you
And I
Sleeping so free
Letting me breathe easy
For I have nothing to hide
Or fear
I just want to be pure
And tall
And lick your ears
And hold your waist
In my arms
Dance in the street
And make love on the farm

You are my secret escape
My passion of fire
My gas station life
So I pump you slow
Filling me true
My woman I honor you
So blood
So bold

Sit with me for a moment dear
There is something
I need to tell you
01/14/10

Tracing the broken pieces
Of the cardboard puzzle
Of life in between
The days of youth
The sky turns to black
Always at the right
Time calming the days heat

Realizing
Realistic with fate
Reading the book
Of destiny
With your breath
Next to me
I am the number nine
Of clubs

The Truth

And so strong and powerful
Like a mis-sile
She came to me
Asked to stay a while
Enjoy a cup of tea
Something to eat
Maybe some lunch at three
Stumbling through this
Planet of loneliness
And desolate
Like some long lost
Survivor of some long lost
Human race
So much came over me
That night I first saw your face
Effervescent colors
Dark hews around your eyes
Electrical cords tangled
My feet
Symmetry
Spiritual alignment
Jumping forward flashes
Falling ashes
And just the ground
We walk upon
Fragile and still
The night held me there

01/18/10

Glory and Time

A dusk darkened world
At every angle of touch
Your freckles glare
The morning
Surrounded by
The curve of shoulders
Under the covers

The blurring blades of hipbones
Like French braids twisting
Our thighs lay
French kissing
Sleeping on a bench missing
Nothing in the world
Cause with you this way
I need no other distraction

Balancing on your limbs
Like logs floating
On the surface of the ocean
My life raft
Your left calf
In my right hand
Another day your loyal man
As we breathe into
The lush green walls
Cause every time
I open my eyes to you
I know I did something right

For now
The next best move
Is just rolling over into you
My jungle gym of limbs
Hair and bars

Swinging past Mars
Up on to Venus
You just kiss my face
Circle my lips with the tips
Of your fingers
Caressing under my skin
Seeing the children within
You whisper

That I'm just a big baby
And just a big maybe
I might just sleep in
A little bit longer

Pulling the covers like jackets
We twist
You turn
The bed cooks
We burn
And it's just you and me
When the world
Washes by

As if life-
Was just some kind
Of secret time warp
Filled dreamscapes
Loving blind
Spilled stories
Glory and time
Mixed with emotions and memories
That begins and ends
Every day this way

As long as I can start and end
With you
I know that nothing else

Really matters
And I know that
The only thing
That really matters
In this moment in time
Is this moment in time

That only truly matters
01/21/10

What I Have Found

So maybe you can be
All that you can be
And then you can be
Scared too
And maybe even a bit
Resentful of the future
You speak of all these
Bountiful meanings
Of forward thinking
And fearlessness
Online but inside
I'm just in a line
Of people waiting in line
Just to get closer to you

So you want to get
Frustrated when
I call you on your shit
Then go ahead
And make a fuss
Be a little girl
And go a muck
Cause I don't
Have to follow
I don't have to lead
If you don't have time
For me,
Then that's okay too
Cause I never pushed my
Way into this relationship
And I certainly don't need
To push myself to hold it
Together

I just really want

To believe that
Your not just another
Woman who's says
They love
When they're just scared
Who's says their in
When they're unsure
Who' says she's a warrior
But is weakened
When the weapons come out

I am looking for a true soldier
And I thought that I found
That in you
Show me what I have found
01/26/10

Stay When They Leave

Indian summer day
Blackened out night
The games I play inside
To want the things I have not
And when I reach the destination
Somehow their value lost
Once upon a time
I could control myself

Got the news today
Of your passing
Your final call for help
So easy in my mind
To find that place
And to really let go

Hard to swallow that
You had the strength
To go through with it
And now here we all are
On the other side
Of the crash
Talking about how
We all knew your pain

Getting lost in my own mind today
So many different voices
Speak; all they at once
Tell me all day long
What they want
What they think I should do
Not even giving myself
A real chance to tell myself
What I really want to do

Just taking time away from you all
The garden again
How I missed your flowers
Sometimes I need to dig
Just to remember what it was
To dig
In the garden
My garden of shame

You keep me safe when they don't
You stay when they leave
Even when the sun dies
You brighten my mind
My cemetery in time
My garden of blame
How I needed to walk
Through your isles today
The warm dirt on my feet
The chemistry of danger
At every door
Unleashing strangers
Manifesting escapes
Oh the soil still taste
The same

Indian summer day
Blackened out night
The games I play inside
To want the things I have not
And when I reach the destination
Somehow their value lost
Once upon a time
I couldn't lose myself
02/15/10

41

Valleys and Corners

And to how fast the sun can fade
The way light shifts the shapes
My mind changes gears
Suddenly everything made
Is too much too take
I need to destroy it
To start again
And again
I know someday
Even this
I will have to destroy
Just to start again

To live in the agony
The vicious cycle
Tormenting through
Season of season
Reason by reason
I surface again with a new goal
A new toy
Pulling the trigger, this decoy
Of love
Blow it all away
Take me away
Far from this place again

For I can't stop my mind wandering
I can't stop this pain
I don't want this to stop the rain
I just need it to keep me going
Keep walking though the rough spots
The unknown valleys and corners
The places when I want to run so far
I must stand strong
And just keep moving on
02/19/10

Bedroom Hangers

It's like god dam how many times
Do I have to tell my friends
And family that
This is the one
And then it's not
How many times
Do I have to watch myself
Lose interest
Before I just give it all up
Or just say fuck it

How many times
Do I become the one
Who is ready but
When we measure up our worth
I'm still standing alone
Finally a world on my own
My word actually means something
Today

Hung up on you
Hung up on us
Better to watch me hurt
Myself
I do it all for you
You want to let me down
Watch what I can do with
This knife and shovel
Dark wheel barrel, dark gravel
Straight to the garden we go
Like within less than an hour
I'm digging trenches
Knee deep in mud
Flinging and splashing
In the rain

The only last way to bury this pain
Just for now
Just for today
I guess this is the only
Way I know left to hide
In the pain
To hide from this rain
Hurting myself again
With you on my mind
Such a nice time tonight
Perfect strangers
Bedroom hangers
Clutter the room
As thoughts of you swim
Through me and these
Wrappers of foil
Ready to uncoil
And burn in this heat
Something about
Losing everyone
I have ever loved just
Makes this alright
For it is in this light
Alone & pondering
That I am truly the safest
For the walk alone
Really is the only way
I know how to go

02/28/10

Man these relationships
Really fuck me up man
Keep my head spinning in circles

Cycle of Love

I was wondering baby
If we could spend more time together
You see I pushed to hard in the beginning
And then you told me to back off
So I had to slow down
But now it's just that
I'm still stuck
In this old little town
And I want to get going
We have so much to see
So much peeing on each other
In the shower
This love can be so much power
If we just nourish it the
Way the trees need to grow
Straight up to the moon
In the night
Sometimes I get distracted
Baby, sometimes I lose the light
And here you are to pull me back in
Just keep me this time
And the next one I got you
I'll give you that pass
God dam I love sleeping next
To that ass
And those lips
Oh honey with you on top
It's the way the world
Spins and you control my every move
Finally a man you've found me
And yes we have too much to lose
So keep this cycle of love
Changing and everlasting
Lets put in another quarter
Start a new life

Lets keep this love going
Keep walking through life
I miss you baby and it's this time
You keep me on track
The next one I swear I got you
I swear to keep coming back
So just come home from the gym
And straight into my arms
If we don't give up
Well have the power of
All those who do bear arms
And tear down the walls of fear
And jump into this spring
The fall of summer on our lips
So much to do and it all starts
With you and I
03/15/10

My Father's Early Signs

These thoughts of concern
My eyes are doing something
The blood keeps coming
And people keep looking
Losing work
Missing steps
I can't stop thinking about
My father's early signs
The way his signature seemed off
Just barely missing the coffee pot
Hitting that corner to the bathroom
Felt that way tonight
Missed a few stairs at
The gym

Not even really being there
In my body
Just somewhere behind
The glass
Swimming in oil
Lost in class
Blurred walls and changing
Colors of thought waves
Am I too far back in thought
That I just don't need to see
Or have we just really gone too far
As a society with this heat wave

In march and the windstorms
That bark, through the night
While it rains up north
And bakes down south
And in the middle of the night
The earth just shakes

My poor planet doesn't know
Which season to show
And I guess wearing these dam
Glasses all day, makes it only worse
Cause my eyes don't know whether to
Squint or to stretch
Something about my age catching up
Eye suspect

I just hope I'm not going blind
I sure hope that's not it
So much of the world would I miss
So many beautiful things
To long for and live for
All the colors of my heart

So vibrant as the yellow bellied birds
Soaring, crimson brushed skies
Hang crooked over dust-toasted roads
And black tarred melting highways
So many windows have my arms surfed
Out of alone, in my own zone
Tranced out by traffic and
Sticky tape on my fingers

Picking away at colorful wrapping
Paper foil at the holiday
Oh what a whole day
Without my crystal
Clear vision today was
I sure hope there isn't more
To come

I sure hope that I haven't too
Much damage done
I hope my planet does know
What season to glow

I sure hope for what reason I am feeling this
Way within

I sure hope the doctor was right
That this blood seeping is just an allergy
In the night, and that in a few shorter days
Life will resume again
The way I like it
To see it crisp and clean
I sure hope within

03/17/10

The Moon & Soon

I really wanted it to be you
I really did
Trying to fit this circle
In the square
Looking out the window
Feel me stare
Into the back of my eyes
As the sun
She's just gonna keep on rising
I know everything's gonna be alright
I just really wanted you to fit
This triangle in the square
This bright flare
In the night
The light
Shadows the moon
& soon again
It will be June
And I will be alone again
And I will be getting older
And these old shoes still fit
These loose lips
Sink ships
While my heart wonders
Truly
Deeply
If I really ever truly have known love
Have I really ever
Known love
And will I ever find someone
That I yearn to keep
Someone that wants to keep me
Something worth sharing
God I really don't know how to do this
03/23/10

51

fuck

Sticky Ginger

Lying in my bed
Lying in my head
Your dark skin matches
My dark mood
Not much food to munch on
In the kitchen sliding
My calloused feet across
The linoleum making
That sweeping noise
Like my father used to make
In the middle of the night
Searching for a plate of
Milk and cookies

Back to bed
Your head, soft
With big full lips
Chocolate hips
And that stick
Sticky ginger
So much fun
The way we connected
Big black rock
In the middle of the
Night, maybe
Just maybe
I will let you
Spend the night
03/24/10

That Steeple Across The Street

So many plans I made
In my head
So many places
I was just making
Lists of things
To do
With you
Everywhere
We were supposed
To go

Like a deer jumping
Across the skyline
Or like spilling
Three drinks at one
Time standing baffled
Confused and amazed
What the fuck just happened
To the last ninety days
We smashed together

I see that steeple across
The street and I know
You see it too
From the kitchen
Cause I'm in the kitchen too
Now were two
The other halves
Back to ourselves again
Back to our old routine

Head down
Hands on my spleen
Picking up where we
Left off right

Before we got scoffed
In the rain that night
In December
Stuck in your eyes

Back to where I was but
Maybe only worse
Cause now I just have the
Memory of your face
Your fingers, the grace
Stuck with just the fantasy
Now of what we could
Have been what
We should have been
How could this happen
This way

This way to abundance
I'm just confused ma
And I refuse to excuse the
Way we could have been
The way we were for a while
Then like sensitive crabs
We scurried sideways
And now the ocean has
Taken us away

Off to the deep end
I was heading
So many plans I made
Inside my head
Amazing how much my life
Changed
The future, the names
So many different choices
And now I change
It all again

Back to having no idea
Not even a clue
What tomorrow will bring
Or even with whom

03/28/10

Priorities

Finally free again
The way I am meant to be
Had to quit that job
And get back to my dream
The only thing that
Makes me shine and
Billow and create
The best day of my life
I don't have to wait
For today I'm gonnna
Fix that old vacuum
Order Netflix
Get a pull up bar
Find a new comforter
Give away my old TV
Drop off some dry cleaning
Hit a meeting or two
The gym for a few
Make some lunch
Maybe finally start
A proper photo album
Of all these Hollywood
Years, the tears the glory
The picture frames I'll need to buy
So many things pass through
These eyes
As long as I know
This is the true me
Then nothing else matters
Cause this is the way
I always wanted it to be
Today I am living my dream
03/29/10

My Black Pirate Ship Remains

What's Easter Sunday
When you live alone
Alarm clock
Telephone

Half past twelve
Half passed the mess
This chess game called us
Been more than a week now
I guess

Its time to digress and play
In the thick mud
Outside my door
The earth shakes and quakes
And I just stay cozy in my
New down comforter

Comforting my life away
Why didn't I buy this sooner
Thinking to myself grinning
Rolling over as another
Missed call passes me by

I guess this is kind of like getting high
Watching the sunset through your eyes
I guess this could be called happiness
Walking naked in my nest
The housekeeper sure keeps
A clean house indeed
Can't even walk through the kitchen
Without every appliance
Smiling and gleaming

Still miss your beaming

Gleam
Watching the water
Run through your hair in the shower
All the power we made
Steaming the windows
Sure could keep this couch comfy
And cozy watching movies

Again in my mind
And on the Tele
Something of comfort and the maze
Hazy and lost in Tuesdays
Of tomorrows
Try to stay centered and not harbor
Another lost love, taken
By another pushing spring, fling

Guess I can get back to my garden
My garden never leaves
She just grows with these bodies
And memories of life
Never too much strife, when I satisfy
Myself this way
A cry for help indeed
Today on the couch I bleed
And weep

For a whole country in mass
Sitting on my ass
So content on a bed full of
Duck feathers, so fuck Heather
And Julie and maybe just
You too
Cause sometimes it just feels
Good to say it out loud
Maybe I am too good for you
Who am I to limit myself

To think that I am not too good
For someone too scared

Strong thighs but easily scarred
By the winds of change
These rusty lovers bars
Tired of shaking them to open
No key, just chains

But my black pirate ship remains
The starboard bow full steam ahead
Through these earthquakes in Baja
Oh yeah and aha, all of a sudden I am okay
With you not in the room
I guess

My nest
This is somewhere between
A total wreck and deep bloom
Content in my room
Stuck on slouch
Falling in and out of love
Somewhere between happiness and the couch

04/04/10

And the losing day   light
Will weep until d a w n
And w   a   i   t for you to come home
Again, the nigh t
Makes th is life

The blades of crisp c u t grass
Only the way you s a w
I   n   h   a   l   e d so deep
Your breathe o n top

The mountain
Luscious and moving
Running through
As seen by the o   c   e   a   n
My world

Let us not forget the sight
Of love won over fear
Of hope slicing
r   e   g   r   e   t
Let us not forget
That w a l k   in   the r   a   i   n
The f   r   e   e w i ll of t   a   l   k
And the pain

The journey to carry u s

On until forever

Again we carry no pain

No   self   will

Just the will from above

Clear skies and the white dove

L i v i n g   o n l y   f o r   l o v e

Words You Whispered

This could be a reflection
Of you and I
Somewhere crunching
In the middle of the night
The power of the moon
Over stapled leaves we walk
Through the misting fog
Rugged boots
Steepened terrain
Cars passing just the same
The water flowing
Rippling rapids
Frozen hypothermia blue blood stiffens
Kitchen screaming, children blistering
Choking this fluid, mouth
Flashing memory of your skin
Clawing into thin air
Just the other room we once lived
The harmony of life completing
This cycle like a tumbling dryer
We tumble
Mumble
Cacophony of death
Remembering the words you whispered
As I smash through the trees
Blood seeping from this knife
Thrashing in my skin
With no escape within
The disease holds me tight
Till the morning
She will come
If I just hold on
Just hold on
Hold on

04/28/10

The Carrier

You call to leave those messages
Then you want to fuck
Then you want to call
And say no more
Use me, sex me, text me
You're just too pure
And then you write a goodbye letter
Then you want to cry
You want to fuck
Good riddance or good luck
Then go for a walk
I think the next call
Should be a doctor
We need to unlock
That medicine cabinet
Drop the net end the bet
And clean that filling head
Take a break from your
Super human altered ego
And just let it all snow, blazing
And realize you're crazy
Fucking nuts
Cause you are
Bleeding hands in a broken jar
And I love it that way
Sick and deformed
Crooked
Like a mental patient
Let me care for you
Subjugate

With my lab coat
I diagnose
Taking your inventory and your panties
Now bend over and take

This dose, show me your wrists
Take off those wet clothes
Through your nose
It burns
As we take these windy turns
Swinging a rusting anvil
Spinning downwards, scathing
Burying memories in landfill
Throwing rocks at the chapel
Cause it's of you
Whom which I need
Our rotting apple
Cause it's from you
Whom which I feed
Like a loony bin
You're stuck within
The way I'm stuck with sin
Writhing hot in roofing tar
Were both trapped in a sinking car
These games we both play so well

05/10/10

We Make Up Again

Spider man lovemaking
I wonder woman all day
Twisted pain subsides
With comic relief regain
Darkened clouds to rain
It's just a marvel this love
We find ourselves sheltered

Like roulette I stay spinning
Changing shapes and clothes
Barely keeping up with a week
Seems only every once in a while
Cardboard back
We match

So we light, we flare
The curtains stare
As we romp, hitting walls
Lotion weeping
It's just your eyes in this moment
That I beg will stay open

Your legs ajar
Our lips, our scars
In moments were closer than
We've been in weeks
So just hold on, slow down
Again from the top now
Show me the ways of love
Eyes open arms ahead

We make up again
To recreate another day
Feeding me woman this way
Like jet fuel in mid air

Amazing how replenishing
You smear all over me
Like a new man I stand
Like all of a sudden were normal
And healthy
And the afternoon
Follows the morning
And this makes sense
And so do your lips
Biting and pulling
Chewing this food down
Out the window the sky
Grows grey
And just maybe
Just maybe rain is on the way

05/17/10

Giving You Away

So long since something
So fragile, so graceful
Has even caught my eye
For so long little bird
My feelings for you, every night
True, everyone feels the glow
My high-school crush
Pinching my sides
Tree moss as soft
Gliding in snow
Every night I ran, in my head

Never were mine
Not even once
Just a few gentle nights
Awoken by your side
Our story goes backwards
Like lie, then the body, then time
Never stopped me
From playing pretend
Never stopped me
From bending these lines

So pretend wife
Let's step into this pretend life
Think about all the seasons
Why this should work
Then the reasons why nothing
Ever seems to happen
The mind plays tricks
On me and you

Well you just order another drink
Stuck to a barstool
Stuck there to think
Fingering tapping your phone
While I'm focused building a throne
And again every night
We both go home alone

I've carried this flame
Brighter and brighter it burned
Tried to stifle it out before
A few times swore that Was
Was the door
The way out and away
But inside can't help but ponder
Is it the one that looks good on paper
Or the one that just feels so good to hold
You see you are the latter
Your neck is my lather
You know it so well playing with your hair
I can see it in your eyes

So I leave town for a few days
My career and my bags I carry
I come home your married
Shocked and sprayed
Lost and dismayed
I thought we were playing pretend
Like a lover I never loved
Lambs lead to slaughter
I'm more like father to daughter
Giving advice not needed
It was all in my head, I concede

So pretend daughter, I bleed
Give me the pleasure please
Of just holding your hand
One last time
Let me walk in line with the organ
So everyone in the pews can see
That I am the man
And you are the daughter
And in loving you
I'm going astray
One last time
In your arms today
You see, playing pretend again
And this time I'm giving you away
05/17/10

To Find God

The rain is here again
It seems natural to want change
Maybe paint the house again
Some vintage thrift store
Shopping whopping
Monuments, framed in my mind
Or on the wall
Which does it matter
I stare at them both all day
Let us play with the present
Moment that seems to warp
Myself, into this ball of energy
Like cool refreshing clouds of
Rain, maybe a drive to the ocean
Is intact today, just to watch
The waves break away
As I know a strong year
Of triumph is here again
And there's a mountain
I am about to conquer
And I guess I am preparing
For what or who lay
Rested and bountiful
On the other side
For that one single moment
As all pain and fear subsides
And I know the path has
Once again lead me to
A suspended moment
Of peaceful bliss
And just the mist
Of the ocean
Is all one needs
Sometimes
To find God
05/18/10

Hold Us Together

Ran into you tonight
Funny how with your mignon
You slow and glance
With your girlfriend
I dance, with two
We enter
Are you with a bunch of girls
You ask me
Task me, a label
Make me something
If you want to see, me with you
Ask a question
And watch my answer
Time stamp, clamper
The summers coming
And I think I already
Jumped trains
My love
A few days already
And I haven't had the nerve to call
Guess were running out of
Sex with nothing else
To hold us together
Heavy as guilt but
Light as a feather
I guess this relationship
Just might be floating away
Light as silk
But hard as leather
The fact that I need more
Too much to take
Without boundaries it's hard
To fake this happiness
So when you ask me
If I am with a bunch of girls

What do you think
Is happening
What did you think would
Happen when you pushed me away
Heavy as guilt
But light as a feather
Take this letter as a falling
Barometer of mercury
And just for the sake of me
Please carry on like you really
Don't car cause it's too dam
Hard for me to pretend
That this doesn't hurt
When it's all I can do
To not let it eat me up inside
I wanted this to be with you
So bad, but now that I know
It's not let me cross this
Crosswalk and eat in a place
After all this was my restaurant
First, so thirst, for a Thai iced
Tea somewhere else please
And let me walk in peace

05/30/10

Stickers In The Sun

Like sea salt when it settles
We just wave gently back
And forth with the ocean
Bodies wrap like a pretzel
Sticky icky weepy sleep
Every where I turn
Our limbs churn
Melting together
Like play Doh
Knees bend the wind
Hips join a boomerang
Reliant slip-knots
Giant kiss-bots
My elbow under your frame
Your cuddle muffin
My mane, fingers
Kissing gently
The little silver tongue
Slithers out
Sticking and stabbing
Like a baby rattlesnake
You rattle
Until morning I'm saddled
Into your thoracic
Squeaky town squeaking
Us down
This new town, under the gun
They say you're from ninety-one
Give to me your lips
Take them to this suture
They say I am from-the-future
And when we come together
It's like some kind of special love
That was sent from above
And I don't think either of us

Need to understand to feel this
So soft caressing
Hands intertwined
Like mixing red wine
I wake up and there you are
Simple and petite
Sunday morning now complete
Let's just freeze time for a moment
And let the rest of the world
Wash us by
We stay in bed
For way too long
Stuck on each other
Like stickers in the sun
Just can't peel your hand away
Slithered in body heat
We rest in summer's deep sleep
Like sea salt when it settles
We just wave gently back
And forth with the ocean
Bodies wrap like a pretzel

06/05/10

The Next Shell In The Clip

Covered in your body
I sweat and melt
We blend our bionics
Spirits dance the sacred
Drum beats
As love we make
The sheets we bake
And after tonight
We truly have bonded
No matter what happens
After this
The after life indeed exist
06/07/10

Outside Our City Gates

I hate the way we pretend not
To see each other
In the same room
Sweating and looming
I hate the D and the I
Before the stance
Between us
Drive me insane
The new dance, we swing
Our broken wing

Please bring me back down
From this rooftop of shame
Scaling the edges, tip toeing
Around every corner of my city
Hoping for a glance
In the kill zone, tranced
Waiting for you to hide
Behind your green shades

Dismayed, in the recent messages
You send my way
In broken bottles
So bleached out and blanched
Like they could have fallen from
Some robotic branch
A fortune cookie time machine

"Hoping that I am surrounded
By people that love and care for me"
Well who the hell else would you hope
For, some soft bitten scorn
Wild boar pack of whores
A truckload of enemies
Seems somehow now

Were frenemies, and it hurts
So bad, even when I stare into your
Eyes and you just see right
Through me, acting like
You didn't see, or even worse
You do and just follow course

But then sometimes, you come back
Up for air
My little girl inside
Is there, and you reach for me
Her voice is back, and she stands
There, waiting for me to take her hand
And like the drug addict I am
I do and I stand, in a black suit
Your loyal man, please ma'am
Your taking too long this time dear
The times that I need you here
They're just too far and few in between

Missing your face on my spleen
All I need is just one touch, magical
And I can't remember the dark clouded
Forest, that lies behind my hazel eyes
When you're not around
And every corner I bend it's not you
Every smile I receive is missing
You in three's, that forest that's
Burned out of green trees
Dry and barren in the dark
The creatures on the ground scurry
In the park and steal and throb
And it's hard to just try and sob
And make some kind of healthy
Boundary between the past
And the present

Fallen King to a Peasant
Now I stand outside our city
Walls I once owned
The key and the gate
The whole throne the estate
You once gave me all
Your kisses and soft words
Hands, heart and heels
Now scraping crumbs
Of your attention is today's meal

And I wait still
Outside these city gates
In linen pants and a wool shirt
Rusting shovel in the dry dirt
Waiting for you to take this hurt
And make it disappear
Like whispers in my ears
I just can't feel you anymore
This six months to the day
The rain came
And the little girl
Came my way
Still waiting for you
My love to come home

Staring out the window again
Resting between sets
Getting lost in the sweats
And the music
Watching you across the room
We both share
Remembering the very
First time I ever saw you there
And I wondered, what it would
Be like to be your man

06/11/10

Frame Into Charcoal

What a day
Some spirit from the past
Shown the way
Through your young woman
Frame, the new century
Somehow you have gained
Access too, so you slither
Through, like a girl
Just out of high school
Yet you re teach these old
Tools, the excitement for life
I guess this is why we have
December to May

I guess this is why we have
Somewhere to stay, tonight
Like you said last night
As you sketched my frame
Into charcoal window panes
Like some long lost artist
We all spin in our own
Universe and then we collide
And spin inside of someone
Else's, but like they
Say on TV, everything
Is temporary, so for this
Beautiful cocoon to bloom
Let us sunny hot & perfect loom

I will take your hand in mine
Like a student that teaches
Me back, maybe I will
Sip from your veins just

A wee bit longer
Stronger we both
Seem to be, getting
And letting, things just
Be the way they are
Seems just right to me

06/16/10

Of Value & Core

Saturday morning
Can't seem to rise from bed
Stuck between needing sleep
And needing you more
I been here before
But the sun shines so bright
How could I not want
To run straight into life

Must this stay always
Between us, where
Has our trust, between lust
Been cast away, distant
Stray dogs wander the streets
Of love looking for more
Discerning the conversations
We held over coffee pots
Hand held entrée plates
As waiters just walk
Away waiting for another
Moment in the conversation
To break

Yet still I travel on
Riding a new train young with steam
Not ready to show the world
My old trick still playing
In the background, my secret
Radio listening in the distance
Kissing new lips with guilt
She's so young and fragile
And somehow the teacher
Is healing, while you reveal
A new world to something
So pungent with life

Probably should buckle up
These dirty leather boots
Soiled and mistreated
And walk the solo path
Of manhood, alone
And heal right, seal tight
This self worth
Raise tight these britches
Of value and core
Search for the teammate
Worthy of water and nutrient
Trimming the edges
Of life and find this
Greatest fern in the tropics
Fulfill my love of self
With the love of you
And complete this journey
For two, where life
Truly can begin again
And love shall overwhelm
And over shadow, hobbies
And chores, blanket even
The tallest of doors
Only to cast the biggest
And warmest shadow of comfort
Anyone could ever ask for
In a single moment
My whole life makes sense

06/19/10

Thirty 4

What a great day of self love
Filled with fulfillment and desire
Share the meeting with
The liar and the disease
It is at ease today
Thirty-four reasons to keep
Them all away
Just a massage & corsage
For me and you
He plus two
Add eight more
Finally a dinner with friends
We made this year
Feels so good to be with
My best friend and nineteen
Sponsor, friend's teeth gleam
Chinese food and great laughing
This year was a great day for
Passing the good times
Hell yeah thirties are
Good times
06/21/10

Just Burning The Edges

Feeling so good today
So much empowerment
In the free will I choose
To distill this goblet
The life that I lead is
Truly the life I love
Writing on the walls
Again today
To be anything
That I want to be
To go anywhere
We can be ourselves
To see the world
Lets plan today
A trip somewhere
Far, far away
Lets get lost
In the airplane
Line, the backpack
Signs that lead to travel
The only road to inner
Redemption, self-preservation
Indian reservations
Of tranquility of peace
Let us be blessed children
That our parents dreamed of
Instead of resting in peace when we
Pass on let us rejoice in the comfort
Of soft fleece and joyous freedom
Of choice and free will
Let us travel this world like a wheel
Spinning and ever unfolding
Vibration-al thought waves keep
Pulling through these flames

06/28/10

Into The Sun

The river runs dry
Near the far end of the hill
The looking eye darker
Than before, the hour
Still clocking more
Shocking and dismantled
Carrying this bag of memory
Searching everywhere
For your scent

Somehow, disconnected
We have lost touch
No longer seeing your face
No clothes, no legs
Can't even find the magazine
This month, so prove
To me you exist
Prove to me this
Wasn't some final-fatal
Fantasy still believing
In me, the days ahead
May contain our laughter
And strides

Was such a dream to see
You, there in the night
Dressed in black robes, black tights
Boots and lip-gloss
Long hair and gloves
How the rain can wash
The city away
Why can't I find the courage
To call you back my way

Still needing you, the night

The new door opened
And substitutions in place
Newer music, newer face
But it's the comfort in the mess
I guess, searching for activity
And nothing less, than the best
I just don't believe in bad timing
I believe in you and me

I believe I am the fool
Again because I believed
All the words you spilled
The days you thrilled
And put me, through
The times we made
Love, so true

Watching you cook
In the kitchen
Burned into my hands
My forehead
Now looking at what
Was the present, now past
Burning this paper heart
So fast, where have
You gone into the sun

07/02/10

Showering On Mute

Taken pills swallowed down
The wind charred leaves brown
The eyes to see
Through the darkness
The room clouded and grey
Filled with so many voices
They stay all night long
Yet just for a moment
It's you and me
And I can see you strong
See you so clear
Like a child in my arms, yearning
To grow, like life a lava lamp
Changing shapes with the heat
Melting and pulling
Falling and peeling together
Why can't I control
This overwhelming back
Flipping into tomorrow
And sliding out of today
The arrow points this way
Through the trees
Gloating its floatation
Into my arms puncturing
Ripping sinews from
Car seats to the oceans shore
Racing towards you even more
Pushing the line forward
Every night I perform
In dialects and destitute
Showering on mute
Washing me clean
From this day dream with
My eyes wide open
Life is harder now than it used

To be, getting confused
With the pages of my life
I have to keep them in order
Neatly stacked books
Of lovers and schemes
Nightmares and dreams
Here for you all to read
And weep, steal and seep
Into the night like thieves
Always searching for love
Like my mother
With a shovel, with a knife
Starving for the heat from life
And passion, the hunted
Forever an artist
Victimized from the life
I lead before, the stories
My guides putting me
Through, even somehow
You belong right where
You do, finally reading this page
It's true, life brings you, to moments
And beats, that you're just supposed
To hit and see what they hell
Is on the other side of that fence
Or wall, standing still in a stall
My dreams just behind the door
Everything a thought wave
Even pain and glory
Your panties and my worry
About bills and car accidents
This truly all is just
A figment of our spiritually null
Imaginary lull, towards center
Eternal desire for
The fire of salvation
Emancipation declaration

Of a knife worth giving
Of a life worth living
Yearning to enter
The cave of redemption
07/02/10

Down The Back Stairs

You were always on my mind
Today I found the way
A door way out
The limp noodle
Of sex drive finally
Connected the dots
Back to a heart
Feelings have been restored
And you are now free to
Roam around the cabin
I hate goodbyes
So for this is
My way of saying it
Goodbye and take care
Be well and die hard
You were one of
The greatest
Short lived
And crazy, just like
I like em

07/07/10

Linger For Long

Broken glass shatters
Back stabbed
The way home in blood clot
Trails to the morgue
It is what I still do best
Strapping you in the chest
With fatal mortal sized wounds
Rounds filled with nitrates
To soak your blood
Cause it's like the old game
'You hurt me, so I destroy
It all from the ground up'
Pulling
Falling
Again aching
The knife between my legs
Slices you apart
Destroy what was left
Linger for long
Something so pure
So white
Now drenched in blood
And disgust
The way I leave the place a mess
You just can't help but scar
By this charring nature
The nurture of dysfunction
Keep our motors wheeling
On hot engine oil we function
Like coffee brewing in the morning
I stay awake all night, just
Hating myself even more, digging
Deeper trenches of shame
Guard the light
The name of the game

Escapism
When I was just a little boy
Looking for love
With blood on my hands
And everyone crying
Trying to leave
Now awake a man
And once again broken
Another heart
Even my own
I slice so smooth
Waiting, watching
Towards the front of the room
Asking
Please send someone please
Come to the rescue
Only to be laid to rest
In these pages
Someone please come
To my rescue
To find these idle
Hands, digging
Sinking
Deep in muddled lands
Ruining your weekend
And our dream plans
Some sort of fantasy ending
No boundary
No definition
Just hurt, and pain
When my mind wanders
Back to your face
When your mind wanders back
To our place
I can't help but wince
At how bad things really got
Un believable

Where we got off
This train wreck against the wall
Bodies scatter the hillside
Crash and burn we fall
Helpless, distant, we fail
07/10/10

Intentions & Aspirations

I tried to walk away with integrity
Save some of my fragile heart
For the next one
Never acting out
Never wanting to hurt you
I have waited for so long
They say its progress
Not perfection
They say its lag time
In the direction
I guess I get so bored
With the monotony of healing
That I have to re open these
Healing wounds
Pouring salts and irritating
Them to the point of infection
Watch the dissection of our friends
After I make my next move
Making sure you can't come back
This time it's horrible
On a scale of one to ten
In horrible ways to end things
I would say a fifteen
Horrible feeling
Quiet and reserved
At the bar
Needing a bar or more
Walking through the flames of life
Knowing that I started out
With great intentions, and aspirations
To be a better stronger man
It's the way your shoulders hold
Your head
The way your eyes pierce
The skin

You are my sin, I just can't
Say no, I never want to let go
Tattoo it thirty seven times to my body
I just can't let you go
I just won't let you go
07/10/10

Salt She Stings

Fingers to the heavens
Arms spread wide
Tidal waves
Going deeper
White foam
As your black bikini bottom
Moans, jumping up
Like imaginary jump rope
Ducking these swells
Glistening hope pushing
Afternoon rays reflecting
Shimmering listening skin
Looks like the tides
Coming in
Looks like my mind
Wants to grow dim
Don't have to follow it
These days
I can let it run astray
Even if it goes far
Far away
I stay here on the beach
With you
Getting smaller
As these gigantic swells
They breathe
Reaching for us
The oceans salt she stings
Your hair blows
A girlish scream of joy
Our crashing waves deploy
As dreamy sandcastles
Gently come down
As these gentle waves
Drape you in a gown

Swishing wishing
Smoothing the sand away
Looking down at my feet
The veins crawl further
My own fond memories
On this beach
So many things to distract
Me, up there
In a darkened mind place
In another dimension
Of time and space
How many levels of life
And spaced out living
Can we restore
Like a giant closing oak door
Smearing layers of thought
Waves over the lines
Auburns and limes
Watercolors and time
Falling from a string
Through the sky
But slowly
As if weighted down
Breathing with my throat
I stay down here afloat
Safe and the sand
Resting with my hands
Content
My heart
And will set free
Watching you run
And jump with glee
As nothing else can see me
In these
Summers breaking waves

07/25/10

The Weakness In My Armor

Giant heaving hips
Calves and thighs full
The brim of your skirt
It flirts, while my eyes
They tell you
Of all the things that I have
Already decided we will do
Undressing you I do
Watching that Champagne
Go drown
Go head girl drink it down
Let that heavy alcohol
Take you away
Cause its just the shoulder straps
That'll go away
As the bathroom walls we hit
Pulling your skirt up looking
In the mirror those pillows
Of love with my face I splash
On my knees we clash
Sucking lips
Hands down your waist
You tug at my pants
Yes baby, I will feed you
Yes we will dance
The hotel room tomorrow
Littered with clothes
Sucking the blood and ice
From your thighs
Your panties of rice paper
Like sushi rolls I pop them
Cracking you, deeper
This is why I work so hard
To work you out so hard
You big, big girl

You currently rule my world
I just can't stop this way
Your big ass takes me away
Suck these lips
Spread these hips
Let me slide up inside
Of you
Take us both away
Let the champagne flow
And take us both away
You big fat cow
You're a juicy hamburger
And I eat away
Smiling like the Cheshire cat
Against the wall
Pervert, I
08/28/10

Dusty And Worn

No I guess I don't trust you
Even though I want to and
Possibly could
If I really let go
Bt then I would have to stop
Making it snow
Urges
The twinges I get
In the weeks to come
The darkness undone
That shovel
Against the wall
It gets dusty and worn
And then the storm comes
Followed by the scorn
Of a woman
The solitude of no

I am the moth

You are the flame

Face Just Sinks

Walking home in a mist
Just feel the city
Kiss, my skin
The club cars rolling stops signs
Preying cop cars, skipping white lines
Passing the street
We walked our first night
Like stepping in water wearing socks
Feeling the pain seeping
Through walls
Curtains smudge black
Floorboards steep, creep
Under these city streets

It would never be the same
I never knew
The way we met
The hour in your frame
Burns on my hands
Memory sings so loud
The way you created a home
Naming our children today
Throwing away tomorrows
Cause I swear you had your hand
On mine too
The years ago
I dreamt of you
Before you finally came

I never wanted you to know
The biggest fantasy in the land
Your love
My hand, your man
Why couldn't you just
Understand

Somehow I never told you
Scaring so easy to see
The flames you raised
Would eventually burn even me
Like a new family
I would never be able to keep
The days you would turn away
The way I seemed to hurt us so
I never could tell us when to let go
I thought you were that ship
The distance now, your lips
Some goliath rescue liner
Strong bow and full stout
Coming to take me home
After so many years of toil
I spoiled in the fact
I would finally make it home

That cold day
Smoldered flames
February called for love
But we must've
Just missed the call
Somehow we lost touch
With ourselves
And our dream
Somewhere
Someone let go

Such a dreary morning
The day in my gut
I would have to jump ship
Another mid journey test
Like all the rest
My heart just bore and sank
Walking warped and wooden that plank
The wind blown hair

My feet began to crank
Toward
Crashing waves below
Awaiting
For me
To evolve
Back into a little boy
I dissolve

From heaven to hellish mud
Another memory of suspended love
Your tiny hand against my side
The ocean takes away
With lips, your eyes
You promised forever
But I can't find you anywhere
Today
And to be honest I haven't
Seen you in weeks
My face just sinks
The saltwater
As deep under the sea
Falling from this plank
Again I fall free

09/18/10

The Harvest Moon

Quiet, the phone rang and subtle
Huddled answered I
It was Autumn that called back the sky
Under the stars last night
I had to take the roof down
Prance around our little town
Gallant and defiant
Happiness
Stomach fed and heart full
Laughing giant
And rolling my eyes

The way the season changes
The air feels different tonight
And then suddenly
When someone doesn't notice
Like past cuts bled
Just like the lights that turn to red
Life has changed
Again
And today we befriend
A totally new place
And palace of mind
Our platform or time
On the planet

Wherever you are
Right now in this very moment
This is your home

In the night we lay naked
The places we keep
Those that stay sacred
Different sounds
Different drawers

Yet somehow it's still
That same front door
Same front stoop
Yet changed and absurd
Totally different
Mind and picture frame
Don't make it sound lame
Cause its not; it's more
Fantastic
Than before
I'm wrapped in plastic
On the floor
Intrigued and beleaguered
Indifferent

And bewildered
The way that teenage girl
Wrinkles the sheets
Falling in love with my first
Four legged, counting sheep
Now begging to see them both
And the wrinkled sheets
Jumping to fall back
Into safer thickening sleep
Again in my arms

That morning when
The alarm arms
The dew separates plants
From the ground
The soft unspoken sound
Go easy on the sizzling bacon fats
Heavy on starches and proteins
Of birds awakening and then
That mean, loud
Rattling hum of the Mexican
Gardner and his drum

Las Palmas awakes like
A squeaking summer screen door
As we all bang and pour
Around pots and pans
Coffee pots, night stands
Round and round again
One more time

This time will be different
Yet somehow we know
So here's the first throw
We awaken
And just like last night never happened
Hungry, thirsty for a new day
I look up and taste the sky
Autumn has followed us home
09/22/10

All This Hair For You

All this hair for you
I just sit here
Staring at you
Braided hair like yours
I can still see through
Your pores
Watching you prance in
With all your ten years of glory
Looks like the story
That used to be the one
Before we became one
Hot pink flash pants
Your so adorable
You flash dance
In the steamy windows
Of the humid sunlit
Sky smiles then cries
Dark shades cover the dragons
In your eyes
Possessed since a child
The world in those thighs
Oh blinky someday well make nice
They say if your walking on thin ice
You might as well dance
I know one day well have another chance
Hair sticks to my neck
& shoulders
Wiping across my face in the morning
Still lingering
A memory here
& there
In mourning
So long, brown, soft
Watching you stretch out
Like some ballerina performing

Im sweating away before you
I know you don't see me honey
I guess I can't see you either
Were just one and one
And two
Different people
So I'll just finish my cardio
And stare at you baby
Just keep doing you
And stay true
Been growing for so long
All this hair for you
10/10/10

Waiting for Coffee

The cranky lawn mower rattles by
Like a helicopter smashed sky
Cooling, tooling, building
The Empire of my eye
Feeding ingredients
My pie
Bakes in the Californian sun
Crisp like the sound of your heels
Tapping along the roof
Watching your hair fall from
Your shoulders to bed
Resting my head
Your chin understands
My subtle win
The times you lean in
To kiss me
To the trees and the sky
And must I let another day
Pass us by
Let our relationship settle, subtle
Like wine an oak barrel
I need this bone to marrow
And aim the sights back at myself
This suicide mission of life
Envision, enlighten, and fulfill
The road that God has paved
I drive any car
He borrows me these scars
To see my growth
It is all growth
Rasping my throat
Crushing crunch
The leaves of Autumn bring
Me back to my favorite girl
Oh December you always

Run my world
Warm colored scarves
And winter boots
Keep me warm
When the snow falls in my mind
I must let go
Of everything in due time
Allow another growing full
Tomorrow backs into my life
Where is my wife
No one asks
Me as If I still ask to myself
Who cares these days
Inadequacy labeled
Lighted and asked to leave the room
Snickered, I've got so much
I want to do
And always
Falls into place
The order of the day
No matter how I seem astray
God has bigger plans
For you and me
So squint in
And burn the sun
Feel the hum of the city
Today
As I stretch and overturn
Over ran and wide churns
Well paid, (add) overslept
I dreamt of a life
Well-lived last night
How joyous
Today
In my eyes and in my dreams
This is my means

11/03/10

The Blessed Curse

Loving the way your voice
Rattles through my phone
Pushing one just to hear
You again, so full
Vibrant, uplifting & spirit
Talking so soft
Lips like moss
Of the great Oak tree
Under the moon
Soft, your skin
To me, in the morning
Mika my love comes
Running after long sleep
Under the bed, she just
Can't leave your side
Your shadow, her pride
My two baby girls
Sleeping at my thighs
The way God graces me
With woman
Must be the blessed curse
Of the world
Reaching over
My new world
Just lays there
Waiting, watching
For my marbles to wake up
Look around and smile
Hearing the jingle
Dragon lady comes to life
I kiss & snuggle
Shiver & huddle
The softest arms
For me you reach

11/03/10

Dumpster With The Alley

Crickets & cockroaches
Scurry under the shadow
To the corners of the garage
My car park, ready for bed
Large as the garage door wide
Aluminum rivets bend
As the giant wall falls, toward the floor
Scuffing my boot, the hallway
The complex behind, metal gates
Stepping over the heat wave
The way the bees lay dead, and dry
On the floor
Watching one or two
Survive the meltdown
Crawling around their
Fallen comrades
Swollen heat waves
Cause them somehow
To lay collected and grounded
For life, in my hallway
Short lived lives
I walk past and mourn
For a blink or two
Then back to life
Just, as we all do
Subtle moments that flash
Corners of my eye
Play tricks on me
Things that aren't really there, we see
Feeling the things we try but just can't flee
Striving & stretching toward thoughts
We wish, hope and yearn to be
Eating and living our own memories
The sky finally cool
Like wet wool

On shoulders
In my hands, tools
For boulders and clams
To open treasure chests of life
Surprise myself with so much
Positivity, I ponder
If anything could ever go wrong again
Or maybe just my perception
Has changed & the problem
Remains the same
Change your perception
Of the problem
& like your love, once again
The problem is gone
Alone to the dumpster
With the alley, I bond
Midnight chores
Soon my neighborhood snores
Walking past the old parking spot
Thinking mighty how hot
It is tonight, feels like summer
Walking past the grave yard
Of bees in the hallway
My breath leaves
What a bummer when
The sun screams
When the bee stings
& just the pile to walk around
Tells the temperature of the room
Tonight leaning November
Pushing forward every dimension
Even through death
We all bloom

11/05/10

Breath Of Fire

Eating from your mouth
Dipping spoon
Our tongues joust
Teething about
Pushing lips
Inside her mouth
Black hair everywhere
Persian princess help clear
The blankets
And smooth back the sheets
Paper machete hips
Red hues from
The cross dips
Across my back your fingers
Tucking away behind my mouth
The way the black shark sleeps
In the dark streets, coveted
Awaiting a devilish return
Awakened, adjourned
Babies sheltered in polyeurethene
Styrafoam bedding holding frames
The bull whip, a head dress
My calves gently laid rest
High above the ground
Covered red bedding
Above the sand for miles
My Persian princess sleeps
Weeping, laughing
Sheltered & shinning
Fragile frame aligning
Under my core, finally atop
We find each other, in alignment
The confinement of two bodies
Heating each other up
Like trapped in a snow bank

We bank on each other
To keep moving, going
Until we braid like hair
Our bodies melt in air
We hold here to stay afloat
Keep holding
Let me my stray
Bend the wind
Away, like the ocean
Or even better a calm bay
With this night
Coal black Persian hair
Let me float away
Just laying back
On my back looking up at
The night stars
Watching the world
Pulling away
Into a sea of abyss
The red room dissipates
Blurring, slipping
Your little narco dissolves
As I unravel the walls
My mind leaks
Blackness on its own
Floating myself away

11/13/10

Black Rubber Lips

Oh mimi's kai some kissys
Just please, pretty please
God, I miss your knees
Your little white feet
Scattered all over my floor
Bending down to fill your bowl
Yes I have treats my lil girl
Everywhere we go
Daddy and mimi time
Leave mommy at home
She has dishes to do

I just want some kissys
Please, one more time
Around the block
Ill let you smell everything
You want, just come when I call
And sleep when I cuddle
My baby girl, shuffle
We dance in my arms

Like a baby I cradle
Oh my little princess
I miss your toes
Rubbing your belly grows
On your back now you trust
Face to face I thrust
My lips against your
Little black rubber lips
I wanna feed you every meal
Our love baby girl is real

Just hurry and come home
Cause I really want some kissys
My mimi's I can't go too long

Without you, now that we're here
We must go everywhere
I wonder what your doing
When you're all alone, come
To live with me and ill give you
Your own thrown
Pink little tongue licking

Long white hair everywhere
Somehow love has taken over
And I just don't seem to care
That everything black
Is now a shade of grey
I wish everyday
My manager would let you stay
Cause I hope mommy doesn't
Get too jealous, but I love
When we have our own time

I never loved a little girl
Like this before
Oh my little mimi's
You're running through
My world
11/29/10

Fifteen Adorned

Sitting here thinking
December eleventh
I probably
Should be drinking
But that would be another story
And then this wouldn't make
Much sense to me

Make more sense to me
This year, my life
The jar, every time
I shake it and step afar
Different colors shift
To stars, the smell
The memory always feels
Different, like books
That age, the pages
Wilt and fade, yet
Somehow even dead
Of the night, tonight
Your smile still burns

The way you wear
My jewelry, I can still
Feel your stare, you
Think of me too

And for that
I color us both blue
And spit these paint balls
Against the wall
Watching the way the colors bleed
Into my mouth

Passing your house
I can't not; turn to think
Stop to stare
Sometimes I dare
I still want my share back
Part owner in this company
Looking through your
Pictures like
Pressing down
On broken glass
The pain of asking

The stain and masking
Tape to cover the seams
The places where I never
Painted your trim
Wondering if that purple
Still lives on
Smeared and sponged

I'm right here behind you
Hovered and lunged
Were both doing our hair
Pretending not to feel
Black tights paint your thighs
I can still see my son in your eyes
And I am afraid you just might
Too, a relapse for two
This season for you

Oh December, like
The wind and the glass
You cut me & my past
Shoveling us along
With the snow
I try to not let it show
But Cancer baby to the core

I can't lie, I can't ignore
The artist inside must
Bleed, I feel

I have taken the time to heal
I even stayed strong-
One year, no smoke babe
One year, still I choke-
Slaved
Wrapped in scarves, I brave
The new day
Walking forward I know
I must keep going
But it's dam hard today
To not fall to my knees
And whimper

The ways I still wish it were you
Somewhere, deep in my mind
I'm still sitting here with you
My heart
On the porch keeping you warm
Making out like we're fifteen
Adorned
Hoping
For nothing, except
Falling asleep to your charm

Waking up in your morning arms
The birds and the bees
The sun comes through the window
Even the sky looks the same

From your place
So close we live
Yet so far we stay

One year ago today
Just for a few minutes
I'll let the pins and needles flank
Loving you
Sitting here blank
I remember
The eleventh of December

12/11/10

Velvet Cloak & Choke

Obsessing over you
Again, fuck
I'm through
I took that first hit
And now one is too many
How many times
Can a person come un done
How many times
Do we have to play
This dumb
Who were you then
And who are you now
What were we supposed
To be

Yeah I loved you, so what

Yeah I stuck to you
Like a cut, only seven
Months later I had to leave
Town, tinseled frown
Chiseled down, my core
Sweating, your beeping
Back door, pink bra
Pink floor, the pirate
Seas now rest calm
Kissing French we
Rest calm

Talking gibberish
To myself, like my father
Did before the winter
He passed
Sipping coffee at night
At last I am completely

Delusional to want to go back
Where there was nothing
To stay for, speeding away
Once so hard to do
But finally reached
Why must I look outside
Of myself to be complete
Selfish competence, defiant
Radiance
Overwhelming
Smoldering love
Hovering doves
Burning the wings
With flames, with smoke
Take a velvet cloak
& choke yourself to sleep
For you are a façade
You are my armor
Dressed and bribed
By some sucker who lied
I am not my thought
I am not my poem
I am not my muse
I simply exist
A window frame
In lime
A thought of a man
This is just
My eight-year-old hand
A tiny grain of sand
I guess this is just
You combing my mind
This is just one tiny
Moment in time

12/13/10

the secret to life is to love

.

the secret to love is to live

Sometimes you need to walk the city at night

To feel the city breathing

To let the city in

Sometimes you need to walk the city at night

To feel yourself breathing

To let yourself in

I Won't Be Hemming

Sometimes I need to walk
To feel the city breathe
Late at night
Watching traffic whiz by
The dark irony
Of life
It's the homeless
Who go to bed early
Up curly with the sun
Now blanketed
Drunk & doomed
Under the watchful eye
Of the moon

That place where the old
Wells Fargo ATM used to be
The Staples business refuge
For the wind, biting hard
The night skies beauty at large
While my feet ache from
Another long day
So long have I stray'd
Losing sight of the city
Inside of a day
Sometimes I need to feel
My life walking home, I stay

Walking home alone
The cold
It's real
Letting the city
Breathe me in
Learning to put love
And myself in the same sentence
Putting up with sin

Needed to get out
Of myself tonight
Wanted to fill the void within
Watching your aged legs
Spill out of your dress
Splashing over your chair
Like a hunter I
Smell lust
It's right there
Within her hair

Plus I slept way too long today
Amped up and charged
Into you like a barge
I push
You pull
We drip
Eyes closed
Like vampires
We thirst
My bedroom
The great hearse

Splashing dance floor
Winded brown & soft
Yet, suddenly I'm lost
In missing my own lover
Like waking up with no covers
Cold, now curious
Fantasy expires
Desire is gone
Like a balloon pop
Instant drop
Stop & roll
And just walk the fuck away
Needed to get out
Of myself today

Walking home to feel the streets
The city I breathe, within
Pasta boat stuck on TV
Outside CNN
Glued to the way
The world looks this way
Passing the places
Where she walks
The zone; I used to call it
I guess now it's
Just down the block
Whatever & however
Were all black birds
To a flock, the mother
Of tick & time she tocks

My desires' stock, crumbles
Like the dirt beneath these
Shovel's heaves, the winters
Tree's leave
Barren & skinny
Just fingers to the sky
Pointing out the places
Where I used to get high
This void inside, just needs
To be home, no death match
No throne, the garden tonight
I thought I needed
But instead, I just needed to feel
The dead, of winter
And the city breathing
Cold concrete
Beneath my feet
No harm no foul
I'm going home where it's safe
And sound, where I
Can't & won't hurt you

Where the sky stays so blue
A place where the void
She can rest in fleece
And I can whisper feelings away
I guess this is showing up
I guess this is growing astray
Noticing the times
I reach outside of myself
For an answer I can
Only find in Him
& how the hell do
I get off this page
Back into my own skin
How much more on this earth
We call time, we find
The one meaning of life
Within
Begin
Overwhelmed
With questions
I stop & settle in

Don't need to answer anything
Tonight, just some warm clothes
& my bed, I guess instead
I just needed to feel the din
I just needed I guess
To let the city win
Like a tiny rip at the seams
I won't be hemming
I'll leave it there for show
Tonight outside with the streetlights
I guess I just needed sometime
To stretch, to reach
To allow myself grow
1/11/11

All The Angels

The rain she whispers
Outside my kitchen window
Like so many days before
It's amazing how fast
The pussy willow tree grows
One day she's naked
The next she's dressed
For dinner saying hurry up
Lets go
All pink buds closed
Waiting for the sun to open
Her up, like my girlfriend
She puts up
With my mood swings
The severe weather
Sings, us to sleep
Alarming for residents
Of Los Angeles to
Get so much rain
Almost gives a pinch
Of the pain, as it reminds
Us of the life we left behind
To come and play in the sun
Under the hum of the freeway
All of us in ways, dreamers
Lost astray in songs from the
60's of Rock-star dreams
& hippy love making scenes
Were the ones that sang a bit
Too loud, we danced a bit too
Strong, most of us
Yes, we stayed high for a bit
Too long, as well
But not too high
The swells today

The ocean in the rain
Looks like my mother's refrain
Making sure I don't do anything
That she wouldn't approve of
Still looking for the white dove
Of love, to come perch
Gently on my shoulder
Lift away the boulder of guilt
& shame from a lifetime
Of taken and greed
Saying yes till we bleed
The citizens of Los Angeles
We are all the angels of the world
Resting peaceful again
Comforted between
Four warm walls, as the gas
Heater clicks back on
The Christmas Tree
Still in song & the sound
Of these keys clicking
Keeps me ticking
As another rainy day
Comes along
1/02/11

SPECIAL THANKS:

Thank you to all those that continue to inspire and uplift me.

Those who take my calls throughout the days when I seem to be
overwhelmed with fear, my support group in recovery
& my family and friends.

You all envelope the only things that truly matter in this life.

www.ingramcontent.com/pod-product-compliance
Lightning Source LLC
LaVergne TN
LVHW041320080426
835513LV00008B/531